The Truth

I believe one of the worst ways you can destroy yourself is by feeling something so truly, so deeply and deny yourself of your dreams

All because someone else who does not have to live with your regrets wants you to

Yet here I am.

Gasping for air,

refusing to breathe it.

Longing for life,

refusing to live it.

When they fail to understand you

try to understand them

When you fail to understand them

try to understand why

These are the rules we must follow in a
world where everyone is competing for
their opinions to be valid.

Lately, I've been thinking

nothing really matters

Not the sun, stars, moon

and certainly,

certainly not me

and not you

Then I ask why

and my mind sobs for

whatever the truth may be

Remember
for the both of
us my
darling
innocence
can be lost
but it may
not be
found

for you
may have
saved the
village

but you still
slain the
beast

When my chest is filled with unforgiving angst, I must wonder if it is because of the side of me who was told to care...

or the side of me who was taught not to.

Isn't it the best to be so incredibly happy,
that you forget you were ever sad?

Isn't it the worst to be so terribly
sad, that you forget you were ever
happy?

This is what it is to be human,
though so many of us are stuck in
the middle just waiting to feel...

anything.

The world will not always give a great example to follow. Neither will the people we love most.

It is up to us all to learn only the valuable lessons taught.

This could be something real great,

if only it were real

Sometimes,

you don't realize something hurts
until you touch it

Like scars or memories

Same thing, really

The days slip by

        slip by

           slip by

And the only thing I have to keep me
company is the thought of yesterday, the
thought of tomorrow.

I'm the girl
who laughs
at
everything

I couldn't
tell you
why

I try to
shake it off

play it like
I'm stupid

I have these
walls

this defense
mechanism

To hide the
pain in my
chest

the lump in
my throat

the
screaming
in my head

The goal is to wake up and strive to be the best we can be with the knowledge that we are not.

It's odd to think about childhood. The

simplicity of everything made it so sweet.

You didn't know how your snow globe

formed dazzling music. You didn't pay
any

mind to the cigarette butts on the ground
and

the second-hand smoke you breathed in

sitting in the back seat.

You didn't have much thought on
marriage,

children of your own, or how much
coffee

would be consumed for the rest of your
life.

You didn't have the basic math, science,

history, biased opinions, longings. You
were

so unaware of what makes life, life.

The magic slips away a little bit, doesn't
it?

When you're aware of the bad around
you or

when something mesmerizingly beautiful
can be understood. Or perhaps when you
not only

love the smell of coffee, but you can't go
on

without it daily.

One heart break after another and you
still

manage to feel just a speck of wanderlust
for

whatever is out there because surely it
must

be magnificent. Surely something

magnificent. Something that brings the
magic

back into existence, pumping it through your

veins.

It's something we all want and something that

can't be looked for. It is fate and it may even

be fleeting but it is the sole reason we all

keep moving and why others give up because

it feels so unattainable.

Do you ever feel like you're in
pursuit of a phenomenon?

I'm always so busy turning every
which way, trying to make sure
I'm in the clear that nothing ever
happens to me.

They sell us perfection like it is heroine,
never caring if we die for it.

At the end of the day, I'm still me and you're still you. The grass is still green, the sky is still blue.

The Hurting

You are the reason anytime love reaches out
its hand, I turn and run like hell in the
opposite direction.

The tears come hot like they've been
sitting on a burner and are finally boiling
over

I turn the stove off and push the pot to the
back

Who has time for feelings?

It was simple in that moment

I needed to be touched

Just to make me forget

Just to remind me

how to feel

all at once

It didn't do me any good

in the long run

I'm not going to lie to you

I did the bare minimum today

Expected results I am not going to get

Not even close

I'm tired

Tired of trying to convince myself this is
enough for me

and I keep praying behind my messy car
and messy hair,

I might be a beautiful person

Sometimes it dawns on me;

this might be all I am

A tired, worn out mess

You said you'd love me forever

I shuddered at the thought

Forever is a long time

you should just let me go

Have you ever tried to convince yourself
something isn't real?

I'm pretending by day, losing sleep at
night and in the morning

it's hard to feel

Whatever you do in life, don't pretend to
love

when you've no intentions,

just don't.

The sin

though young

was not pure

I wish to say it was

There is so much I wish to long for

I miss missing places, people, and feelings

Our parting did not hit me like the ton of
bricks it was

I've been coming to the realization for
some time now

        that I am disappearing

        much like the memory of
        you, of us

   And damn,

     there is nothing that leaves you
     more empty than gradual
     heartbreak.

When it comes down to it, there's not so much we can do about a lot of things. No matter how unfair it may be, no matter how much it hurts.

That's where God comes in.

You told me I was sweet

You said that I was better, that I'd be
better than you were

and my daughter would be better than
me

You asked me why I was so
weak, and it cut me really deep

Out of everything you've said to
me, the bad was all that ever stuck

I'd try to explain to you again

but I don't have that kind of luck.

People say if you want to be
happy, decide to do so and you
will be

But after forcing a smile on my
face

and saying good morning when
I've only wanted my bed

Repeatedly wishing for a full,
happy heart and

thinking it into existence, all to
watch it crumble before my eyes

Well, if you figure it out, let me
know.

Way too young to be this empty.

Everyone keeps begging me to
"get used to it"

But I'm not ready to be this tired
of life,

I'm only 21

You're broken just like me

There's only one difference:
I'm trying not to be.

A body is a clumsy little thing

with a mind of its own

Made entirely out of single celled

crumbs of life

All brainstorming

for your skin, mind, and
muscle in order

to instruct them to feel,
think, and move

Whispers to your core
how to be

Your soul is ideally in consensus
with this

Mine, apparently, did not read the
handbook.

No matter what storm you're
weathering

sprinkles or a hurricane,

just know the rain always stops

You ran through me like I was a
race to win

You never looked back to see if I
was hurt

You took your prize

You left

I almost turned around but
then I

remembered all the times
before

and you've always had a
knack for

making me want to leave

making me want to stay

Best to just let it be

The Fighting

My whole life, I've been taught to
be the victim

I used to think it was because I
was weak

Now I know it was driven by the
fear of my strength

which has the ability to untether
truths, truths that have waited too
long to come to light

and all I've got to do is flip the

switch

And so, I gathered your faults

and your flaws in a failed attempt
to escape mine

I kissed your lips to wish everything
back to how it was
Or to how it could have been
had I done some things differently
or moved and spoke less solemnly

You deserved better
maybe even just something different

Because it wasn't just me
We both ran
head first, onto each other
Throwing insecurities ruthlessly
back and forth

Clumsily picking each other up
Loving and hating equally,
until there was
nothing left to fight for

Until it hurt to muster up anything
but nothing
Until I was done

I hate to admit it, we were the same.

She was too many things
all at once
She raged war in her mind
The world was her battlefield
Her body, her fortress

It would be too easy
to say she was some sort of
beautiful, fiery chaos

No

She feared everything
including what she was
capable of

When I was little

I imagined we were stories

and somewhere way up in the sky

far, far away

we were being read

Most of my adult life has been

based on getting that imagination back

I'm losing sleep trying to forgive you,
trying to forget you

There is so much hate in my heart
burning red for a man I've never
known

for a hand I've never known

the sting of when it's angry

But these eyes

These eyes I know are not all mine

and that alone

kills me

Something keeps telling me to go
for it

Maybe it's all this anger boiling
in my veins

maybe it's the love

maybe it's this hate

What will I tell myself when I'm
old and I didn't even try like hell

to be all I can be

to give every ounce of who
everyone thinks I am up

and become my true self

What will it do to me

to walk on this earth breathing
until the end of my time

only to work towards someone
else's

wishes?

I always think I was happier

before

I always think I'll be happier

after

Very seldom does it cross my mind

that I might be happy now

I have trouble keeping up with the little
things

I feel as though I'm rewinding and

skipping through just searching for

something spectacular when it's now,

life is right here right now

And somewhere in the future I'm either
happy or sad

and about to die

But I pray by that time I'll be blissfully
aware of

life's little nothings

and how they're actually everything

How do you tell someone you love

you're drowning on air

That even out of all you see around you

you still sometimes wish you weren't
there

How do you tell them

you're drowning on air

Its filling up your lungs and

no one seems to care

You're choking on anxiety

the fake smile is splitting your cheeks

You're in a spiraling depression but

everyone just thinks you're being meek

You're drowning on air and

everyone just seems to stare

No one will know if you don't tell

until it gets to where you can't bare

Because of all the breathing

you're drowning on air

How do you tell them your heart is still

beating but you're barely feeling

alive

The air fills your lungs

every second it burns

How do you tell someone who loves you

You're drowning on air

.

The Numbing

I'm at the bottom of the ocean or
at the very least

I know the weight of it

I can feel it

the way the pressure blows my
body

My fat shoves my muscle and
breaks my bones

squeezing my veins until they pop

crushing my organs until they
burst

tingling the tips of my toes

my fingers reach in response

my eyes widen

I gasp

panicking for air

silently

It's 8:42 a.m. and

I smile as if nothing is wrong

There it lay between us

a double-edged sword

We were spine to spine

you pushed

I pushed

until we stabbed each other

and ourselves in the back

Nobody believes you when you say it is bad until they witness you break.

You stood over me

knife in hand

complaining of your red

stained carpet

Water me down and let me sit over night

Pour me down the drain in the morning
and

never think of me again

When given the chance to save myself

I always go back for you

Why is it that no matter how much you
burn me

anytime flame threatens your flesh

I come back to drag your scorched body
to the river

and set myself ablaze

Why is it that I'd rather engulf myself in
your wrath

than to watch you suffocate yourself

I used to ask my heart to be still

"Simmer down", I'd say

when a gleamy-eyed stranger
came my way

Now I beg of it

"Please do something,

anything."

but it doesn't skip a beat or fasten
its pace.

You taught me how to be alone

at a time I really needed someone

and for that I'll forever be grateful

I cannot recall a time I did not
have you in my head

Remembering is too exhausting
and I think I'd like very much to
let it go

The nightmares are making me
tired even in my sleep

These thoughts they always find
their way back like a disease

I wish I never knew you exist

a monster like you

If ignorance is bliss

knowing is pain

and I know too much

It was a school day

I was sick but my mom wouldn't let me
stay home

You invited me to play games with you
and friends

you were the only one there

You taunted me like I was a child

I was a child

You played me songs I can't listen to
anymore

You

You made me feel important

You kissed me like I was important

then you hid me in your closet

We had to go but you were still on the
hunt

You asked if you could come over

said you had nowhere else to go

I snuck you in through the front door

There was no one who cared to notice at
the time

You said my name like you recited it in
your head

to get it just right

You said you love me

You said this is what love is

You said you were only trying to love me

You said you were sorry if you made me
do

something I didn't want to do

Not like it mattered so

I said I wanted to

Then I washed you off my body

scrubbed and scrubbed

still felt dirty

I cried

Your actions were excused

my feelings were dismissed

.

You took something from me

I never knew I lost it until now

now that I'm sitting here alone in the dark

trying to fall asleep but I can't because

I had coffee at 7:00 pm and coffee keeps
you up

I needed it to do school work

I worked

forty hours a week then came home

to work some more

and my question is:

Where did you put my child hood?

Sometimes I can't get you out of my head

the way you

smell

taste

feel

I never want to want someone

as bad as I wanted you again

Oranges make me happy

I buy them often to promote my
happiness

Then I let them sit

and sit

and sit

and sit

and rot along with happy

Come and let me love you

My love is like no other,

I swear

Oh darling

I'll love you until I don't and

when I don't

I'll leave you wondering why

Oh honey

you won't be mad at me because this,

this is all I've been taught

Oh please

come and let me love you

Don't you find it strange

how little time we have

here and how much of

it we spend wondering

why we're here at all?

The Loving

Do rooted flowers wait to be picked as I
do?

My love sprouts quick, red, and
thorny,

and waits...

and waits.

He was a fleeting kind of beautiful

One which could only be caught in the
first morning light
and once again for a moment with the last
glow of the moon

Mine one second and gone the next

Oh, but how I loved him

I don't want you to love me like the movies

I prefer the detail of books or the realness of a live band

If we are going do this,

I'll accept nothing less than your faithfulness to coffee

Or the way you ache for places you've never been

I don't want you to love me like the movies because movies end and people forget

Instead, read me like your favorite book you can't put down

even though it's 3 am

Listen to me like I'm your favorite band

Breathe me in like your morning cup of coffee

Cross me off your bucket list

I knew letting that kind of love in

after being so deprived would

flood me from the inside out,

sinking everything in my wake

        and a drowning person

            doesn't think about

        who else is drowning,

            but of the lack of

        air in their own lungs

So, I did what any other

respectable, self-loathing

person would have done

              I let you go

There you slept, and I wanted with every ounce of me to love you like I once did.

I don't want to stumble through this life feeling hungry

I want to taste the world

I don't want to drag myself through each day feeling even more empty than the last

I want to be full to the brim with outstanding love

I don't want to be a hopeless hoper anymore. I don't want to walk blindly into each day

wondering what it'll be like. I want to be here while I'm here. I don't want to stare up at

The sky longing for something to happen. I want to make it happen. I want to fly.

Unapologetically.

And when it's over, I'll shoot for the ground and watch the fireworks.

Once you look into mirror eyes,

your world will never be the same

You'll find blue, green, and
purple

can all be put to shame

Because the sky, the trees, the
grass, the flowers

have got nothing on your brown
eyed

powers

And just as the world has a
reflection in you,

you have a reflection in my world
too

There are so many reasons to reach for
you,

       now that you're out of my grasp

If my arms don't feel like home if
my lips

don't taste like forever

don't lie to me

and say we are clever

If you can't swim in my eyes if
my thighs

don't send you shivers

don't pretend to be a part of me

like an ocean to a river

If my words don't sound like a melody, if

my tone-deaf singing doesn't alter you

don't instigate my beliefs

and fabricate they falter you

People aren't choices

You can't choose them

like you choose between ice cream

flavors

Pick vanilla and change your mind

after you've finished half of it and

trade it out for mint chocolate chip

Sure, you can bask in the sun and

howl at the moon

but do you find yourself gawking at

the sunrise or wanting to chase the stars
and

maybe you'll find an occasional spot

where the ocean and the mountains meet

but don't you dare tell me the water
kisses you

the same way as the trees, also,

would you rather listen to Chris Stapleton

sing about drunken sober love or

read a novel by Hemingway about a man

forming a bond with a fish he wants to
eat and I'm sorry but

I find it amusing that life

does not always offer up a golden

person who

no one can hold a candle to and

when it does, we try to strike matches

watch them burn out, get second best

all because we always think there's

something better

.

Are feelings real if they are one sided?

I'm jealous of you for the way you are
loved by me

Sometimes I feel I should have the
audacity to

take some of that love back for myself

Then again, who am I to deprive you of
such love

What good would it do for me to look at
it in the

mirror every day when I could see it
shining back at me instead

I want to be as present as air

flowing essentially so that others
may

breathe my being

in and out like a mantra

Infinitely providing for the bigger
picture

loving every minute of it just
because I'm there

I want to be so free I become out
of grasp

there enough to blow the leaves
on the trees

and keep the supple of your skin

I want to be here without having
to think or worry

to have one solidary purpose:

to just be

Since you
got out of
the water,
the ocean's
not been
the same

Suddenly
the only
fish in the
sea is me

.

He

was a monster

The worst
of his kind

I fell in
love with
him, still

The way
you jump
out of a
plane

For
amusement

For the
rush of
knowing
that with
the slightest
mishap

you might
not make it
out alive

It is the
possibility

of fatality
in which
drives us

wild

Like fire
burning
through the
woods

All things
happen for
a reason

so they say

.

When you picked me

I warned you I have thorns like no other

I warned you

no matter how you removed them

or how long they'd been gone

still they would linger

the sting would grow stronger

Most beauty has consequences and you

owe a great debt to me

You see

when you took me from my roots

I was only just a bud

I pricked at your hands begging you to
stop

now I've bloomed, and petals are falling

out on your counter top

The water you've given me, the glass
vase

is nothing

compared to the home I had

And you cry out only for yourself

When you whimper

it is not for the selfish

love you bore from me

but for my dry, crumbling thorns

inconveniencing your life

.

I could not make you come where I was
going

For where I was going, your heart was
not

But if you would've asked me to

I would've stayed,

I would've stayed

When I went looking far and wide
to be all I can be, wouldn't you
know I found myself standing at
the edge of the sea

Don't say anything

I might be leaving very soon

Ask me where I'm going, I dare you

The answer is everywhere

We only have one life after all,

don't we?

She throws her curls back, giggles and stops my world from spinning

What a wild child she is when she's just woken up

She is everything good and everything right, I would like to keep her just as she is

I pray for no harm to come her way

She snorts and I want the world to stand still for one moment longer

There's something stirring in the world.
Something dark. Something light.
Something wrong. Something right. Who
are you to yourself? Who do you want to
be? Are you bad or are you good?
Everyone has a misconception of both.
We are here, living. Living beings who
are renting earth for a short period of
time. There seems to be lines we've
drawn on land, in water, the sky, feelings,
meanings, religions, where does it end?
Do you ever stop to think we need to be
unified?

I felt eyes on me

It was too hard to avoid

those eyes on me

Mine fluttered up

and back down

when I saw her eyes on you

That's the problem with people like me

we fall in love with the idea

Sure, I loved the idea of loving you

just like I love the idea of never eating
cake again

It's a romantic thought

Not very realistic, but romantic

That's not to say you can't be loved

or that I can't love

just like I can quit cake if I really, really

wanted to

I'm just not ready

I'm sorry

I went searching for galaxies in the ocean

I didn't find what I was looking for

but I was in no means disappointed

You make the pain sound like music.

It wasn't like I could have fought for you

You made it clear a long time ago you
would love only yourself

I won't put my love in someone who can't
love me back

If I could marry a Saturday morning,

my coffee cup would never run dry

my heart would always be full

my face would father a hundred more laughing lines

If I could marry a Saturday afternoon,

my fingernails would be forever filled with paint

my robe would stay on as long as I like

my time would only be measured by burning candles

If I could marry a Saturday night,

my feet would remain bare

my music would play for hours on end

my love of books would only grow stronger

If I could marry a Saturday

my, my, my,

my Saturday would look a lot like you

I keep waiting for my mind to catch up
with my heart

so that I may live truly and peacefully
within myself

Love

Love will be there to hold you,

they said

To rock you back and forth when you're
hurting too much

You're hurting too much,

they would say

Love

Love will pick you up when you fall

Unless of course,

you fall too much

Love

Love will help you through the night
when the night is too long to sleep,

you were told

Then Love haunted your thoughts until
dawn

You were told Love would carry your
burdens

The truth is

it won't even carry one

Because Love, sweet Love,

can be still,

silent,

hard

Love will not save you from yourself

Love will stand by you while you try

Dearest family and friends,

I love you all so much. Thank you for all your love and support. I know I have not always been the easiest to love but love is tricky, isn't it?

A special note to my daughter,

I love you more than anyone. Thank you for loving me for who I am and allowing me to do the same for you. You will always be my greatest accomplishment.

Never be someone you're not, Jellybean.

Made in the USA
Columbia, SC
29 April 2019